YOUR KNOWLEDGE HAS VALUE

- We will publish your bachelor's and master's thesis, essays and papers

- Your own eBook and book - sold worldwide in all relevant shops

- Earn money with each sale

Upload your text at www.GRIN.com and publish for free

Rachid Merzouki

Literary criticism

GRIN Verlag

Bibliografische Information der Deutschen Nationalbibliothek:

Die Deutsche Bibliothek verzeichnet diese Publikation in der Deutschen National-
bibliografie; detaillierte bibliografische Daten sind im Internet über http://dnb.d-
nb.de/ abrufbar.

Imprint:

Copyright © 2013 GRIN Verlag GmbH
Druck und Bindung: Books on Demand GmbH, Norderstedt Germany
ISBN: 978-3-656-56829-2

This book at GRIN:

http://www.grin.com/en/e-book/266180/literary-criticism

Literary criticism

By

Rachid Merzouki

Content:

Introduction:... 3

I- The Historical criticism:.. 3

II-The new criticism:.. 4

III- Reader Response theory:.. 5

IV-structuralism:.. 8

CONCLUSION :.. 9

REFERENCES: 10

Internet Resources : 11

Introduction:

Despite all its shortcomings, literary criticism still supplies both the writer and the reader with the tools for self-evaluation and self-improvement. It comes in various forms and for different aims. The evolution of literary criticism passes through different schools and approaches as one school opposes the other. Some of the major approaches that stood against each other based on different assumptions, had been started with the historical theory that was hugely criticised specially by the mid-twentieth century tendencies which knew the emergence of the New criticism developed by Anglo-American writers, and later the growth of reader-response criticism followed indirectly by the structuralist theories.

So, what are the major principals of these schools? how did the new criticism opposed the contextual and historical criticism? How rebelliously reader-oriented theory challenged the 'text'- oriented theories' of new criticism ? how meaning is produced according to the structuralists ?

I- The Historical criticism:

One of the most basic approaches used in the analysis of literary work refers to the historical method of literary criticism. Historical criticism main emphasize is to understand a literary work relying on the cultural, intellectual, and social context that produced it. Behind his or her work, a writer's life and biography is considered to be the first step to analyse the literary work. A historical reading of a literary work starts by examining the various ways in which the signification of the text has changed over time. At the heart of historical criticism, it is necessary for the reader to evaluate a work of art, not only based upon their impressions of the cultural statement being made in the work informed by their own social and cultural history, but of the statements being made within the context of the period in which the work was created. To return to Weldon Kees's poem "For My Daughter", for example, we learn a great deal byconsidering two historical facts--the year in which the poem was first published(1940) and the nationality of its author(American)—and then asking how this information has shaped the meaning of the poem. In 1940, war had already broken out in Europe and most Americans realized that their country would soon be drawn into it; for kees the future seemed uncertain and dangerous. Depending on this historical information, it helps explain part of the bitter pessimism of kees's poem.

II-The new criticism:

Unlike the Historical criticism, New Critics treat a work of literature as if it were a self-contained, self-referential object. Rather than basing their interpretations of a text on the context of the work or the author's life, as it is the case in the historical approach, New critics perform a close reading, concentrating on the relationships within the text that give it its own form.

As a type of formalist literary criticism, new criticism reached its height during the 1940s and 1950s.Precisely, the Anglo-American traditions of criticism in the mid-twentieth century was noticeably influenced by one of the foremost poets and critics of the 19th century <u>Matthew Arnold</u>, who was often regarded as the father of modern literary criticism. In his essay "the study of poetry", Arnold gives poetry the highest value when he believes that "mankind will discover that we have to turn to poetry to interpret life for us, to console us, to sustain us" [1], and he proposed that philosophy and religion should be replaced by poetry. Arnold believed also that modern poets should look to the ancients writers and their great characters and themes for inspiration and guidance. For him only some literary writing should be viewed as 'Literature' then be part of the 'canon'; the idea that will later be rejected by some authors who viewed the canon as being artificial and hierarchical.

The work of Arnold laid the foundation for 20th century criticism of <u>T.S. Eliot</u> which both viewed as reassessment and reaction to earlier writers. His part in criticism is the reaction against the romantic inclinations by rejecting the individual's perfectibility and "Inner Voice". A critic, according to Eliot, must follow objective standards and conform to tradition through respect for order and authority. By achieving impersonality and objectivity, Eliot sought to raise criticism to the level of science.

---

[1]Matthew Arnold ,*The Study of Poetry (1880),* Critical Theory Since Plato

New criticism and the whole of modern tensional poetics derive their strength and inspiration from the writings of I.A.Richards who has formulated a systematic and complete theory of the literary art. His methods had been well described in his famous book *Practical Criticism (1929)* where he reported the results of his experiments, which was based on giving poems to students without any information about the author's life or the context of the work and ask them to write commentaries about their processes of reading the poems. The objective of his work was to encourage students to concentrate on 'the words on the page', instead of relying on preconceived beliefs. Richards argued that criticism should follow the precision of science in order to establish the special character of literary language. Richard's most influential student, William Empson, advocated the idea of seeing poems as structures of complex meanings and separate the literary works from their contexts.

Based on his book, *the well-wrought urn,* Cleanth Brooks highlights the fact that critics should be objective and scientific in their criticism. Brooks said that "critics should not forget the differences between historical periods but forget those qualities those periods have in common"[2]. He believed that New criticism should make universal judgements as poetry does.

Evolving the ideas of Matthew Arnold, which mixed culture with formality, F.R.leavis expressed his opinions morally, believing that literature is the representation of life and texts should be valuated according to the content and author's moral perspective. He attacked late Victorian poetry and celebrated the work of modern poets as *the great traditions.* A literary work, for Leavis, can be understood through 'close reading' without any knowledge of social or historical context. Leavis's approach rely heavily on the construction of traditions that are considered to be the 'healthy' and correct form of English writing.

III- Reader Response theory:

As a direct reaction to the New Critics theory, Reader response theory strongly rejected the way the new critics "wrongly" ignored the role of the reader and stated that the reader's role deserved the same value as the text itself. How texts actually

---

[2] Cleanth Brooks, *The well-wrought urn.* New York : Harvest Books ; Harcourt : Brace and World, 1968.

come to mean something to us was determined, in Reader response theory, through the act of reading. Even if they differ in the norms, the advocates if this theory focused on the importance of the reader and their individual, subjective response to the text.

In the construction of meaning, the reader's approach considered the reader an active agent in the process of reading as he produced the meaning of the work. According to this approach a text interpretation differs from one addressee to another. Each reader gets his own meaning from his own way.

<u>Umberto Eco</u> differentiate between two types of texts; some that are interpreted according to the author's prediction and are closed, while others inviting the reader, decoded in cultural context and are open texts.

<u>Gerald Prince</u> contribution in the reader response theory appeared from his distinguishing of three types of readers; the actual reader who read the literary text and response to it, the virtual reader whom the author addressed when developing the writing, and the ideal reader who understand perfectly the writer's aims. The reader is different from the narratee who is specify in terms of sex, class, situation, race.

As an objective view of consciousness, <u>Edmund Husserl</u> highlighted the philosophical method of phenomenology which is based on the essence of pure transcendental experience. For Husserl the method of phenomenology consists of the fact that the self is an object of reflection and "how to know" involves consciousness. The phenomenological method "is when considerable amount of time is spent establishing and justifying the relevant concept of reflection." [3]

Husserl's objective view of consciousness is rejected by <u>Martin Heidegger</u> who reconsider the subject by asserting that on one hand consciousness projects the world we live in, on the other hand consciousness is also subjected to the world.

---

[3] Macann, Christopher. "Four Phenomenological Philosophers" Routledge, London, 1993.p31

As one of the figures who formed the foundation of reader-response theory is <u>Hans Robert Jauss</u> who seeks to bring a compromise between that interpretation which ignores history and that which ignores the text in favor of social theories. Jauss uses the term "horizon of expectations" which encompasses the social and historical situation of a given time and place, the factors that encounter in a work's meaning.

Hans Georg Gadamer – a Heidegger follower- argues that all the interpretations are linked between past and present and that the past cannot be achieved without the present perspective.

One of the best known exponents in 'reception theory' is <u>Wolfgang Iser</u>. the text's 'repertoire'(as Iser called it) consists of both Social norms, which are regarded as the aspects of the social world in the literary text that regulate how individuals interact with each other, and Literary norms, include those elements of literature which we have become familiar with over time. The elements of the repertoire are activated through the reader's realization, It is the reader's task to put all of the elements of the repertoire of the text together in a meaningful, coherent way to form a meaning that is realized in various ways as it is read by different readers. This later is divided into two categories;' implied reader' whom the text structures his or her response, but he or she also produces meaning, and 'actual reader' who receives certain images in the process of reading, these images perhaps modified by the experience and knowledge which the reader bring to the text.

Rebelling against the so-called rigidity of New critics, the American theorist Stanley <u>Fish</u> calls his technique of interpretation 'affective stylistics'. He gives more importance to the words of sentences in relation to the reader. Fish has a view that reader is someone who possesses a 'linguistic competence', has an internalized syntactic and semantic knowledge required for reading.

<u>Michael Riffaterre</u> –French semiotician- agrees with both theories: formalism and reader oriented theory ; He believes that even the reader is an intellectual person he could not achieve the text's meaning . In Riffaterre's view, in order to go beyond text's meaning a reader must have a linguistic competence that helps him to understand it completely . In his theory he relies on summarizing the reading process

into four steps start from simplicity and finish by attaining the meaning in a chronological order .

In Subjective Criticism, David Bleich denies that the text exists independent of readers. Bleich accepts the arguments of such contemporary philosophers of science as Thomas S. Kuhn who deny that objective facts exist. He distinguishes between two kinds of response reader : the first is the spontaneous one and the second is the meaning which is attributed by the subjective individuality of the reader's response .

IV-structuralism:

Like New Criticism, Structuralism concentrates on elements within works of literature without focusing on historical, social, and biographical influences. Structuralist critics often apply a variety of linguistic concepts to the analysis of a literary text and it seeks to explain how competent the reader is to make sense of a particular literary text by understanding the larger, abstract structures. As Jonathan Culler put it in his exposition, the aim of structuralist criticism is "to construct a poetics which stands to literature as linguistics stands to language".

Structuralism, however, is grounded in linguistics and developed by Ferdinand de Saussure, a Swiss linguist who wanted to move away from the empirical and national style of language.Saussure laid the foundations of modern structural linguistics, developing the science and strength of semiotics, the study of symbols and signs. Broke down the study of language into sections and distinguished between; *Langage,* as a universal system which has an underlying, fundamental structure,*Langue,* the actual language spoken , and *Parole,* the individual speech act. Ferdinand de Saussure's *Course in General Linguistics* (1916) is a summary of his lectures. For him Language is a link between thought and sound, and is a means for thought to be expressed as sound by the speaker's communication of signs to the listener.

The basis of the structural anthropology of Claude Lévi-Straus, the French cultural anthropologist, is the idea that the human brain systematically processes organized, that is to say structured, units of information that combine and recombine to create models that sometimes explain the world we live in, sometimes suggest imaginary alternatives, and sometimes give tools with which to operate in it.

Structuralism is one of the schools that were influenced by the French social and literary critic, <u>Roland Barthes</u>. His investigation of structure focused on revealing the importance of language in writing, which he felt was overlooked by old criticism. Barthes split this work into three hierarchical levels : functions', actions' and narrative'. Functions 'are the elementary pieces of a work ,such as a single descriptive word that can be used to identify a character. That character would be an action', and consequently one of the elements that make up the narrative.

CONCLUSION:

On the whole, the four theories of criticism discussed portrays the non-complete debate and it encompasses the variety of the critical approaches. The evaluation of a literary work differs from one school to the other, passing from the contextual factors, the work itself, reader contribution in creating meaning, and the linguistic abilities that determine the degree of understanding.

As literary criticism cannot be divorced from diversity, no single approach seems invariably successful; moreover, nothing brings finality of judgment and one critic's determination can be undone by another's ingenuity.

In my point of view, there should be no superiority while evaluating the approaches; instead there is some truth in every theory that helps the reader to reach to a text's meaning.

REFERENCES:

Selden, Raman., Peter Widdowson and Peter Brooker. *A Reader's Guide to Contemporary
Literary Theory (2005)*

George Watson's *the literary critics* (1986)

J, A, Cuddon, Dictionary-of-literary-terms-and-literary-theory (England 1999)

I. A. Richards, *Practical Criticism* (London, 1929)

Matthew Arnold ,*The Study of Poetry (1880),* Critical Theory Since Plato

John Lennard, *The Poetry Handbook: A Guide to Reading Poetry for Pleasure and Practical Criticism* (Oxford, 1996)

Cleanth Brooks. *the well-wrought urn,* (1947)

Gillespie, Fosesca, Sanger, Literature across cultures( )

Macann, Christopher. "Four Phenomenological Philosophers". Routledge, London, 1993.

William S. Haney. A Vedic Science Based Poetics: Toward a New Theory of Literature. Fairfield, Iowa, U.S.A, 2000.

Holub, Robert C. *Reception Theory: A Critical Introduction*. London and New York: Methuen,1984.

Miha Uratnik,Ujkan Bajra ,Bardhyl Dauti. Structuralism.

Internet Resources :

http://awinlanguage.blogspot.com/historical-approach

http://www.poetryfoundation.org/

http://www.online-literature.com/forums/showthread.php?20089-T-S-Eliot-as-a-critic

http://dlibrary.acu.edu.au/staffhome/siryan/academy/theory_history

http://www.essayscam.org/Forum/17/reader-response-literary-theory

http://literarycriticismjohn.blogspot.com/search/label/structuralism

http://www.guardian.co.uk/science/2009/nov/03/claude-levi-strauss-obituary